SIMPLE HIST⊕RY
A SIMPLE GUIDE TO

WORLD WAR I

1914 | **CENTENARY EDITION** | **2014**

Written and Illustrated by
Daniel Turner

CONTENTS

INTRODUCTION

The Great War or the First World War (there is a sequel!) was a war of epic proportions. It started from a simple assassination, but there is more to it than that. Competing nations, mass produced weapons and big armies made Europe a tinder box ready to explode!

In 1914 with war declared, most people couldn't wait to seek glory. By 1918 when the war was finally over, the world never wanted to see such a global conflict ever again...

TIME LINE

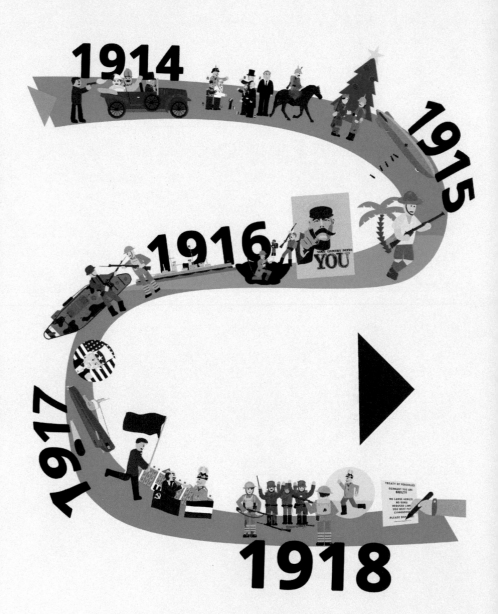

WHAT WERE THE CAUSES OF WWI?

Imperialism

The British empire spanned over 1/4 of the earth by 1900! Colonies such as Australia, New Zealand and India were owned by Britain and made her very powerful.

Germany also wanted an empire, targeting Africa for colonies. Most of Africa had been claimed by Britain and France, so Germany's interests caused tensions.

Arms race

Many nations in Europe had built up huge armies and weapons in preparation for a large scale war. The 'naval race' (competing to have the largest navy) between Britain and Germany, created tensions.

Alliances

Fearing their neighbours, Germany, Austria and Italy formed a triple alliance promising to help each other if one of them was attacked. Britain, France and Russia likewise formed their own alliance.

Mobilised forces 1914 -1918

Russia	12,000,000
Germany	11,000,000
Great Britain	8,905,000
France	8,410,000
Austria-Hungary	7,800,000
Italy	5,615,000
United States	4,355,000
Ottoman Empire	2,850,000
Bulgaria	1,200,000

THE BEGINNING OF WWI
June 28, 1914

The first assassination attempt failed when a bomb was thrown at the car and bounced off.

DAILY NEWSPAPER

ARCHDUKE FRANCE FERDINAND AND HIS WIFE ASSASSINATED

In June 28, 1914 Archduke Franz Ferdinand was assassinated in Sarajevo by Gavrilo Princip a member of the Serbian 'Black Hand'. Franz Ferdinand was an important figure in the Austro-Hungarian empire, and the Black Hand wanted their country of Bosnia-Herzegovina to be separate from the empire.

Britain

VS

France

Germany

Austro-Hungary

Russia

Ottoman Empire

To teach them a lesson, Austria declared war on Serbia with Germany's support. Because different countries had treaties with each other, they soon started to declare war on their enemies. Russia and France declared war on Germany, and Germany declared war on France making Britain declare war on Germany. Soon there were two teams, the 'Triple Entente' VS 'The Central Powers'.

GERMANY INVADES BELGIUM

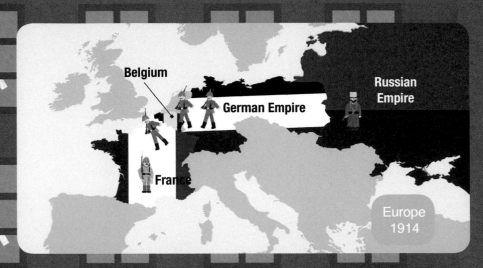

Belgium

German Empire

Russian Empire

France

Europe
1914

August 4, 1914

Germany had 'The Schlieffen plan' - because it was scared of fighting France in the west and Russia in the east. The idea was to quickly defeat France then focus on Russia. But this meant that Germany had to invade neutral Belgium to get to France. This made Britain declare war on Germany.

CHRISTMAS TRUCE

On Christmas 1914, German and British soldiers put down their weapons and made a temporary truce.

December, 1914

Trading cigarettes and chocolate was common

Soldiers sang Christmas carols together

The dead and wounded were allowed to be carried back

British & German soldiers played football

MERRY CHRISTMAS!

1914

ZEPPELIN RAIDS 1915

In 1915 Germany starts using Zeppelin bombing raids on Britain.

THE GALLIPOLI FAILURE
April 25, 1915

Allied British, Australian, News Zealand and other colonial troops launch the Gallipoli campaign against the Ottoman army in the Middle east. Winston Churchill's idea was to lure the powerful German army from the Western front by opening up another new front. By the end of 1915 however, the Allies had to evacuate Gallipoli after numerous defeats.

CONCRIPTION

January
1916

YOUR COUNTRY NEEDS
YOU

BETTER
THE BULLETS
BE KILLED
BY A BOMB

RMY AT ONCE
TOP AN AIR RAID

VE THE KING

In January 1916, Britain started to introduce conscription which meant that men who didn't volunteer earlier were made to enlist into the army.

14

BATTLE OF VERDUN

The battle of Verdun begins, fought between the French and German armies. It was one of the bloodiest and longest battles of the war.

NAVAL WARFARE
THE BATTLE OF THE JUTLAND

The battle of Jutland was the largest naval battle of the war. In fact it was the only major naval battle, which is strange considering that Germany and Britain had been in a naval arms race. The German fleet attacked British ships in the North sea which were blocking supplies into Germany. But in aftermath neither side really won.

May 31 - 1 June
1916

THE BATTLE OF THE SOMME

The battle of the Somme was a planned attack to dilute the German army away from the French at Verdun. The incomptent British commander Douglas Haig, ordered his men 'over the top' and to walk towards the enemy in their attack across no man's land. The British suffered 60,000 casualties on the first day.

Tanks made good cover for troops, and would scare the enemy, too bad they broke down half the time.

Artillery fire could kill a soldier before he even had a chance to get to the enemy.

British soldiers were ordered to charge at the machine gun fire! A bad strategy.

Most soldiers on both sides would carry a rifle.

The Lewis gun, a portable machine gun.

Barbed wire trapped advancing soldiers, if they were unlucky to get caught in it

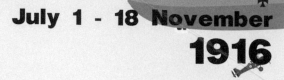

Captured British tanks

German flamethrower

UNRESTRICTED SUBMARINE WARFARE

February 1, 1917

Losing the war, Germany resumes the unrestricted submarine warfare campaign. Attacking American ships bringing food and supplies to Britain caused America to join the war against Germany.

THE END OF THE WAR
1918

Germany and the rest of the Central Powers lose the war
and Kaiser Wilhelm II abdicates.
The armistice was signed on November 11 of the 11th hour
ending the war.

TREATY OF VERSAILLES

GERMANY YOU ARE
GUILTY

NO LARGE ARMIES!
NO GUNS!
REDUCED LAND
YOU MUST PAY
£100000000

PLEASE SIGN HERE!

What next?
As a result Germany signs the 'Treaty of Versailles' in 1919
and is severely punished.

Leaders of WWI, THE TREATY OF VERSAILLES

ANGRY ← → **HAPPY**

Punish Germany!

Peace.

14

Prime Minister Georges Clemenceau France	Prime Minister David Lloyd George Britain	President Woodrow Wilson USA
France had been devastated by Germany. Clemenceau wanted to punish the country severely. He wanted Germany to pay reparations (money) to fix the damage.	The damage done to Britain was less severe by Germany. David Lloyd George was also afraid of the new threat of Communist Russia, so did not want to punish Germany as much as France wanted to.	The USA was the least affected by the war, and saw itself as the peace maker. Woodrow Wilson had 14 points promoting peace by banning secret treaties and letting nations be free from empires.

WEAPONS. & TECHNOLOGY

TECHNOLOGY

Mark I tank

The Tank

The British designed the tank as a response to the problem of trench warfare. The first tanks were very crude and broke down a lot, but these armoured vehicles were soon copied by all the fighting countries with devastating results.

Poison Gas

An absolutely deadly weapon. Chlorine gas was first used at the battle of Ypres in 1915, and mustard gas was used later in the war. If you were hit by a gas attack you would suffocate and choke before falling dead. The solution was to quickly put on a protective mask or wee into a rag and put it against your mouth!

Big Bertha howitzer

Sopwith Camel

Artillery

Artillery pieces were used to shoot explosive shells at enemy positions over very long distances. Soldiers were more likely to die from an artillery explosion than from any other weapon.

Biplanes

At the start of the war, planes were used for scouting, but as the war developed they were used as fighters and bombers. A biplane is named for having two set of wings.

Lee-Enfield

Rifle

The majority of infantry soldiers would carry a rifle. It was single shot, with the bolt being opened and closed by hand each time. Rifles also had to be cleaned regularly because the dirt from the trenches would jam the firing mechanism.

1907 Bayonet

Bayonet

A bayonet is a long knife that fixes on the end of the rifle. Intended to stab the enemy, but also used by soldiers to open cans and toast bread.

MP 18

Submachine gun

The first sub machine gun, called the MP 18 was invented and used by Germany. Holding 32 bullets, it could fire in bursts making it ideal for close combat trench raids.

Club

Soldiers created these close combat medieval style clubs from junk they had around them. With a metal head full of spikes, the club was ideal for trench-raiding and taking out the enemy quietly.

Kleinflammenwerfer

Flamethrower

The Germans first surprised the front lines with the portable flame-thrower. Fire is spread out of the nozzle burning the enemy alive. The fuel canisters on the soldier's back could explode making it a dangerous weapon for the user and his target.

Grenade

Mills bomb

Grenades are small bombs which explode after a few seconds. A soldier pulled the pin and threw it into the trenches to clear them out.

Model 24 Stielhandgranate

Machine gun

The cause of millions of casualties in the war, the machine-gun could shoot hundreds of rounds per minute. Because of the flawed tactic of walking towards the enemy trench, the machine-gun could often cut down entire armies.

Vickers machine gun

UNIFORMS & EQUIPMENT

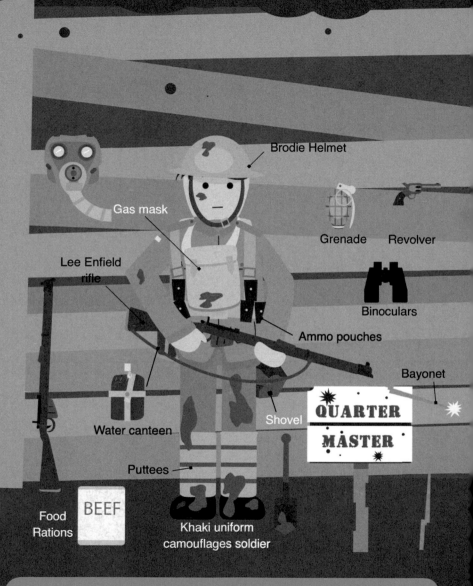

Brodie Helmet

Gas mask

Grenade   Revolver

Lee Enfield rifle

Binoculars

Ammo pouches

Bayonet

Shovel   QUARTER MÀSTER

Water canteen

Puttees

Food Rations   BEEF

Khaki uniform camouflages soldier

Uniforms were made from wool and dyed in a khaki colour. They were uncomfortable and became itchy when infested with lice. Equipment included a helmet to protect from shrapnel, a gas mask, canteen and shovel.

UNIFORMS & EQUIPMENT

Uniforms were coloured in drab shades to camouflage soldiers into their environment (although French uniforms were blue, not much use!)

British   French   Russian   German

Ottoman Empire   German pilot   American   Austro-Hungarian Empire

Bulgarian   British sailor   Italian   Japanese

BRITISH MARK I TANK CUTAWAY

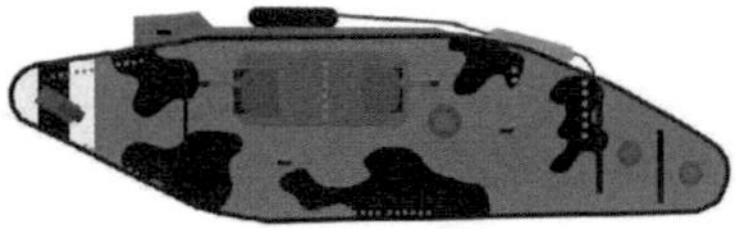

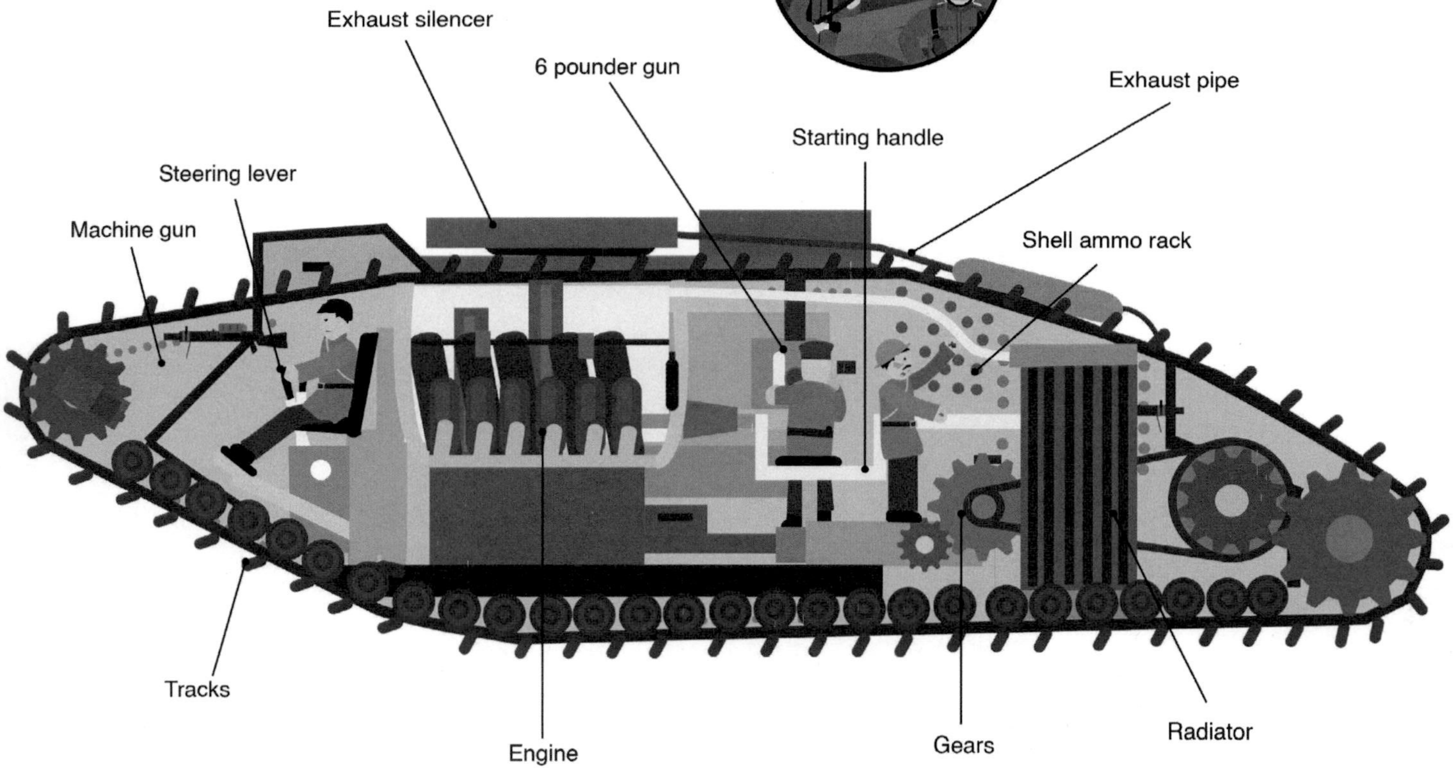

Machine gun

Steering lever

Tracks

Exhaust silencer

6 pounder gun

Engine

Starting handle

Gears

Exhaust pipe

Shell ammo rack

Radiator

THE
TRENCHES

TRENCH LIFE

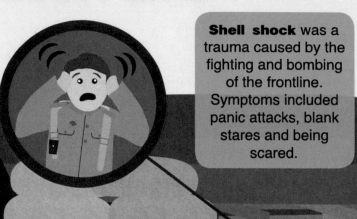

Shell shock was a trauma caused by the fighting and bombing of the frontline. Symptoms included panic attacks, blank stares and being scared.

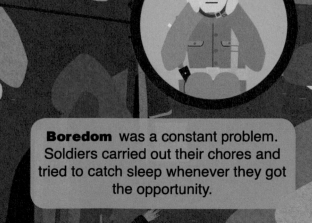

Boredom was a constant problem. Soldiers carried out their chores and tried to catch sleep whenever they got the opportunity.

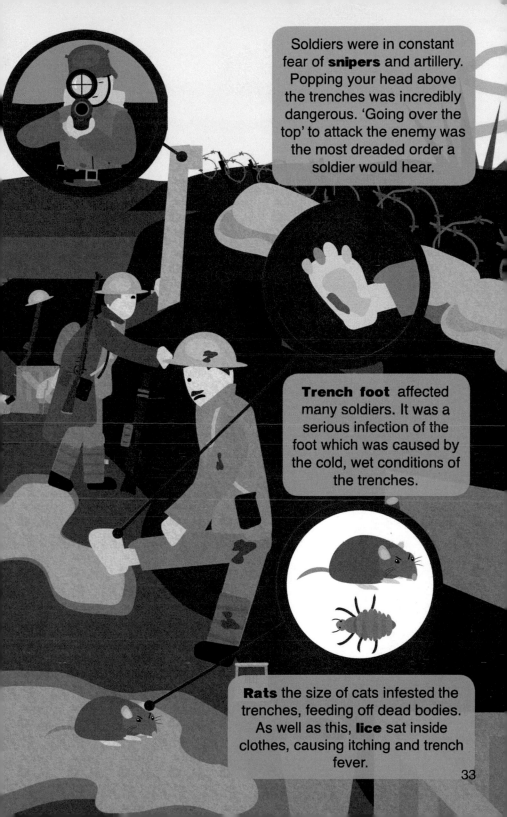

Soldiers were in constant fear of **snipers** and artillery. Popping your head above the trenches was incredibly dangerous. 'Going over the top' to attack the enemy was the most dreaded order a soldier would hear.

Trench foot affected many soldiers. It was a serious infection of the foot which was caused by the cold, wet conditions of the trenches.

Rats the size of cats infested the trenches, feeding off dead bodies. As well as this, **lice** sat inside clothes, causing itching and trench fever.

TRENCH CROSS-SECTION

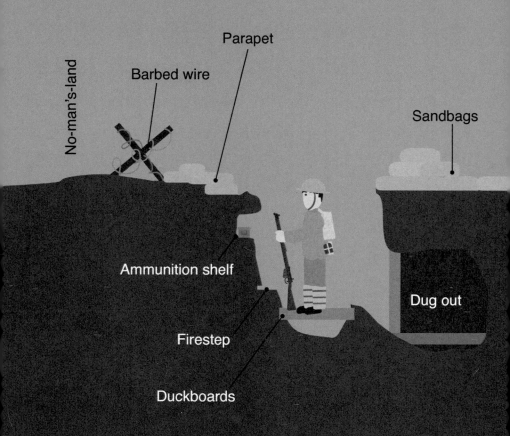

Very early on in the war, both sides dug out trenches so that they would not lose any ground. Living in a trench was a horrible experience as they were damp, muddy, full of disease and constantly bombed by enemy artillery. Trenches were dug in a zigzag pattern so that if the enemy entered it, he could not shoot straight down the line.

RATIONS

These are the daily rations of a British soldier in 1914. Food had to be rationed so that everyone had an equal share in times of food shortages. When there wasn't enough rations, soldiers had to resort to eating dead horses and rats!

BEEF

1 1/4 lb meat

3 oz. cheese

4 oz. bacon

5/8 oz. tea

4 oz. jam

1/20 oz. mustard

1 1/4 lb bread

GILL RUM

1/2 gill rum

8 oz. vegetables

S

P

1/2 oz salt 1/36 oz. pepper

2 oz. tobacco

AERIAL COMBAT

FLYING ACES

MANFRED VON RICHTHOFEN

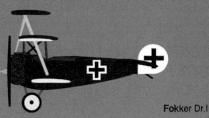

Fokker Dr.I

German pilot Manfred von Richthofen painted his plane red giving him the title the 'Red Baron'. He was the top ace of the war gaining 80 air combat kills.

RENÉ FONCK

SPAD S.XIII

René Fonck, a French pilot was the top flying ace for the Allies gaining 75 kills. He was a great shot, taking down 6 enemy fighters in a day. He survived the war, unlike Manfred von Richthofen and Mick Mannock.

EDWARD 'MICK' MANNOCK

S.E.5

Serving in the The Royal Flying Corps for the British, Mannock downed 61 aircraft in his career. Even more impressive considering he was blind in his left eye. The ace always carried a pistol which he said he would use on himself if his plane ever caught fire.

DOGFIGHTS

The earliest use of planes were for scouting out enemy positions. As the war progressed, both the Allied and Central Powers mounted machine guns on their aircraft, creating deadly dogfights in the skies. The most famous flying ace was Manfred von Richthofen or the 'Red Baron' who shot down 80 enemy aircraft!

Flying aces were celebrated as modern knights.

The Red Baron's Fokker Dr.I triplane had 3 sets of wings.

Machine guns could fire through the propeller blades without hitting them.

Parachutes weren't allowed as they were seen as cowardly.

HOME FRONT

PROPAGANDA POSTERS

Propaganda posters were everywhere at home. They persuaded people to do all kind of things for the war effort, including enlisting into the army and making then feel guilty for not doing so, not wasting food and buying war bonds.

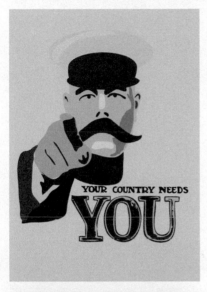

BACK HOME

Civilians were under threat from German bombing raids.

Posters inspire people to join the army and the factories.

Soldiers sent letters home from the front to loved ones.

YOUR COUNTRY NEEDS
YOU

The Home Front in Britain saw women taking over the jobs of men, rationing and civilian targeted bombing. This would transform the nation forever..

So many men were fighting on the front that women were recruited into munitions factories and agriculture, to keep the war effort going.

Rationing was introduced near the end of the war to combat food shortages.

THE GREAT WAR STATISTICS

The First World War which people thought would be over by Christmas, lasted for 4 years. It had killed millions, and destroyed nations.

28 JULY 1914 – 11 NOVEMBER 1918

OF THE **65 MILLION** MEN DEPLOYED TO FIGHT

50% WERE KILLED OR WOUNDED

WWI TOTAL CASUALTIES

MILITARY CASUALTIES: 9,720,000
CIVILIAN CASUALTIES: 8,870,000
MILITARY WOUNDED: 19,800,000

ALLIED CASUALTIES
TOTAL MILITARY DEATHS 5.7 MILLION

CENTRAL POWERS CASUALTIES
TOTAL MILITARY DEATHS 4.02 MILLION

FIRSTS:
TRENCH WARFARE
PLANES
TANKS
SUBMARINES
WIRELESS COMMUNICATION
POISONOUS GAS

FLYING ACES
80 KILLS -MANFRED VON RICHTHOFEN (THE RED BARON)
75 KILLS- RENÉ FONCK
61 KILLS-EDWARD MANNOCK

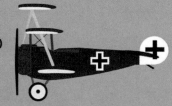

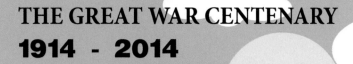

THE GREAT WAR CENTENARY
1914 - 2014

We remember the First World
War with the poppy symbol
because they grew on the
bloody battlefields in the
aftermath.

Quiz ?

1) Where was Archduke Franz Ferdinand assassinated?

A) Vienna
B) Sarajevo
C) Budapest

2) Why did Britain declare war on Germany?

A) Germany invaded Belgium
B) Germany invaded Russia
C) Germany invaded France

3) What was the only major naval battle of the war?

A) Battle of the Somme
B) Battle of Jutland
C) Battle Ypres

4) What was one of the longest battles of the war between the French and German army in 1916?

A) Passchendaele
B) Battle of Marne
C) Battle of Verdun

5) What was conscription?

A) When you were forced to enlist into the military
B) When you signed a treaty
C) When you received food rations

6) What provoked the USA into entering the war?

A) The opening of the Gallipoli front
B) Russia's exit from the war
C) German sinking of US supply ships to Britain

7) Why does Russia pull out of the war in 1917?

A) It has a revolution
B) The Allied failure of the western front
C) Austro-Hungary was too powerful

8) Where was the peace treaty ending the war with Germany signed?

A) London
B) Versailles
C) Berlin

How many answers did you get right?

⌄ 1-3 PRIVATE- Oi! get back to boot camp!

≫ 4-6 SERGEANT - time to lead the men, Sergeant

⁞ 7-8 LIEUTENANT - you are quite the military genius!

GLOSSARY

Abdicate
When a leader steps down from power.

Ace
A pilot who shot down more than 5 enemy aircraft.

Alliance
A agreement between two nations to fight together.

Artillery
Large cannons that shoot explosive shells onto the battlefield.

Armistice
A agreement to end the war.

Black Hand
Nickname for Serbian assassins.

Camouflage
A pattern or colour that disguises a soldier with his surroundings.

Central Powers
Germany, Austro-Hungary and Turkey.

Colony
A country part of an empire.

Conscription
When people are made to enlist into the army.

Home front
The civilian part of the war back home.

Imperialism
When a powerful nation, takes over and owns colonies.

Mobilised
When a country's military is ready to go to battle.

No-man's land
The dangerous area in between two front lines.

Propaganda
Information that promotes action against the enemy.

Rations
A fixed amount of food for everyone during shortages.

Revolution
When people in a country change the current political system.

Treaty
An agreement between nations.

Trench
Long holes in the ground where soldiers lived and fought in.

Trench foot
A disease of the foot from being in damp trenches.

Triple Entente
Britain, France and Russian alliance.

Unrestricted submarine warfare
German navy policy to destroy supplies going to Britain.

Volunteer
Going to fight by choice.

INDEX

INDEX